Slapstick
The Lucy Poems

Taylor Liljegren

Nixes Mate Books
Allston, Massachusetts

Copyright © 2018 Taylor Liljegren

Book design by d'Entremont.
Cover photograph from the collection of the author.

All rights reserved. This book or any portion thereof may not be reproduced or used in any manner whatsoever without the express written permission of the publisher except for the use of brief quotations in a book review or scholarly journal.

Some of these poems previously appeared in *Nixes Mate Review* and in a self-published chapbook.

ISBN 978-1-949279-02-3

Nixes Mate Books
POBox 1179
Allston, MA 02134
nixesmate.pub/books

For my mother and her mother.

"I'm not funny. What I am is brave."
Lucille Ball

Contents

Funny Girl   1

Episode

The Girls Want to Go to a Nightclub   6
Be a Pal   7
The Diet   9
Lucy Thinks Ricky is Trying to Murder Her   11
Drafted   12
Job Switching   13
Lucy Does a TV Commercial   14
Lucy is Enceinte   16

The Sessions — Lucy Ricardo Talks to Her Therapist

Transcript from Session #1   19
Dream Analysis   21
Transcript from Session #2   22
Rorschach   24
Transcript from Session #3   26
Word Association   28
Transcript from Session #4   30

Regression Therapy   31
Transcript from Session #5   33
Role Play: Conversation with the Husband   35

Afterward

Ethel Mertz Reflects   39

Slapstick
The Lucy Poems

Funny Girl

Funny Girl wakes up first,
knows her lines
knows yours
knows the way your mouth moves
when you say something
you didn't write down first

Funny Girl writes everything down first.

Funny Girl has an un-workshopped monologue
she's waiting for you to ask about.

Funny Girl cracks canned laughter for breakfast,
spittakes toothpaste
paints her clown-mouth like a target

Funny Girl will eat that,
drink this, kiss you
deep enough to leave a stain –

Funny Girl loves to leave stains
and call it affection.

Funny Girl is pretty in a way that won't
distract you from the punchline coming

Funny Girl isn't here to explain the punchline coming

Funny Girl will be your mother's favorite
Funny Girl can bake a banana creampie
then wear it like a veil

Funny Girl will jump first, fall faster,
feign sleep when you need her most

Funny Girl won't call back
Funny Girl, "It's not like that"
Funny Girl, "I just don't know what to say
when you're so serious"
Funny Girl, "Why are you so serious?"

Funny Girl will make your uncle full-belly-laugh
at the funeral
will dig her fingernails into her palm
during the homily.

Funny Girl curls her hair
her body

into the crawl space
of your love

Funny Girl always falls in love
falls asleep with the TV on
Funny Girl lets the faint flicker of reruns
dream-dance across her face

Funny Girl dreams about you.

Funny Girl could tell you a story about her father
that would break your heart.

Funny Girl only cries in the shower
Funny Girl tries to wash
the smack of slapstick from her skin
Funny Girl is almost never clean.

ep·i·sode
ˈepəˌsōd
noun

1 : an event or a group of events occurring as part of a larger sequence; an incident or period considered in isolation.
2 : each of the separate installments into which a serialized story or radio or television program is divided.
3 : a finite period in which someone is affected by a specified illness.

"A woman must continually watch herself. She is almost continually accompanied by her own image of herself. Whilst she is walking across a room or whilst she is weeping at the death of her father, she can scarcely avoid envisaging herself walking or weeping. From earliest childhood she has been taught and persuaded to survey herself continually. And so she comes to consider the surveyor and the surveyed within her as the two constituent yet always distinct elements of her identity as a woman. She has to survey everything she is and everything she does because how she appears to men, is of crucial importance for what is normally thought of as the success of her life. Her own sense of being in herself is supplanted by a sense of being appreciated as herself by another....

One might simplify this by saying: men act and women appear. Men look at women. Women watch themselves being looked at."

John Berger

The Girls Want to Go to a Nightclub

The gang agrees to celebrate the Mertz's wedding
anniversary together; the girls want to go
to the Copacabana, the boys want to see a prize-fight.

They see a prize fight. The pleasure
the boys feel in watching another man's
bloodied tooth sail across the ring
is not sexual, but it is
adjacent.

"Maybe, what they've really wanted
all along is for someone to punch
them square in the jaw", Ethel says.

(She is yawning, falling asleep on Lucy's shoulder.)

"I've never been hit
like that. Not for money. Not by someone
my own size".

Be a Pal

Lucy is worried that Ricky is losing
interest in her. When he speaks, he is always angled
away, shows her one side

of his face; his tie, his suit, his pompadour,
obscure him into stacks
of triangles in her mind.

In her mind
he is a shape that loves her. In her mind,
he is a shape that could stop
the loving.

And then what?

Who would I be,
she thinks – walking through Macy's,
watching other women try
on lipstick –
*Who would I be if he didn't love
me? Who is Lucy without
the loving, without the 'I'
of his affection?*

Sometimes when he speaks,
she has this sensation that he could,
at any moment, forget his lines.

Sometimes when he speaks,
she can see his eyes, placard-pulled
away from meeting her gaze.

Sometimes when he speaks,
she swears she can hear the soft choke
of someone else's laugh –

half way home now,
she turns around. Take two.

She will go back and buy the lipstick.
She will buy a new brassiere.
She will buy a book by a different man
on how to win him back.

The Diet

Ricky tells Lucy that she can be in the show
if she can fit into the costume
the dance number requires.

He knows the costume is three sizes too small.

He knows her wanting
is a type of hunger, a thing
her mother tried to train
out of her.

He knows her body is a bag
she will leave behind
when he says the word.

He has said the word.

For weeks, Lucy eats
nothing but celery and her own sweat,
rides the neighbor boy's bike up
and down the steep dark of 68th street,
measures the ebbing moon
of her belly, breasts, thighs

in inches; Ricky watches his wife leave him.

When he holds her in his arms,
he feels the space between them grow
like a child should. That month
when she bleeds, there is only one day
of a deep brown stain. Dead blood.
The mud she makes
of herself washes out
with cold water and hydrogen peroxide.

Later, Lucy looks
at her uncensored self
in the bathroom mirror – holds the soft flesh
of her belly
like a hand.

Lucy Thinks Ricky is Trying to Murder Her

Engrossed in a mystery novel,
Lucy becomes convinced
that Ricky is planning to kill her.
Ethel reads her cards, confirms
her suspicions.

That night, Lucy dreams herself into a long knife:

whenever dream-Ricky touches her dream-body,
his dream-hands bleed.

In the morning after he leaves for work,
she lights a cigarette in bed, smacks
at an itch beneath her pin curls,

"I always do that", she says out loud,
"I always make him into God."

Drafted

Lucy believes that Ricky has been drafted,
which prompts her to weep though

inside she feels the burnt-orange of
a smile brimming beneath
her teeth –

she will never forgive that
foreign wars remind her
of her childhood;

of women building bombs; of blowing
out candles on cakes.

Job Switching

Ricky and Fred are agitated about the girls'
spending, which prompts the gang to swap roles.

The girls get jobs at a chocolate factory,
eat the shame of unwrapped praline;

the boys stay home, make too much rice.
The sin of excess.

Later, Lucy must use Ricky's toothbrush
to make herself vomit. It's brush head is larger,

and it can touch the back of her tongue, her tonsil,
and her uvula simultaneously.

When she is empty, she uses the same brush to clean
her teeth, spits a paste of tooth polish

and blood into his sink. Her mouth tastes clean
and metallic. Her mouth tastes like a man.

Lucy Does a TV Commercial

When Ricky is given his own television special,
Lucy is determined to be on it
despite his wishes that she stay
out of show business –

this is the premise of their love:
want and unwant:
set up, punchline.

Yet it's the first time that Ricky begins to understand
the particular way his wife has been starved,
the particular way she will never be fed: it is said

that when Eve ate open-mouthed our first
sin she began
to understand the edge

of herself. Of him. Of their on-set garden.
Of the way he looks
at me.

It is very funny, watching a woman
fail like that –
to see someone else try

to drink from an empty bottle.
Here is the joke: she drinks too much
of the tonic she's asked to sell

sour belly burps a blue-stream of bad copy
over live airways –

he takes her shoes off first when he brings her home.
Carries her bride-body to his bed.

(She is yawning, falling asleep on his pillow.)
He will hold her all night this way:

smell the sour apple stench of her skin,
fall asleep on the stain

her face
leaves behind.

Lucy is Enceinte

Lucy finds out she is pregnant,
but Ricky is too busy for her
to tell him.
She decides to use a song request at his club
as a way to give him the news.

When he realizes his wife is having a baby,
Ricky forgets his own name.
The lyrics to every song he's ever known vanish.

There is only her
and the affection he feels towards her.
'I love Lucy', he will tell anyone
who listens.
He makes her name into a title.
He makes her name into a song
that everyone can sing.

The Sessions

Lucy Ricardo Talks to Her Therapist

"Every one of us is shadowed by an illusory person or false self. I wind my experiences around myself and cover myself with glory like bandages in order to make myself perceptible to myself and to the world as if I were an invisible body that could only become visible when something visible covered its surface."

Thomas Merten

Transcript from Session #1

I think I'd like to talk about what is grey.

About chocolate and *arroz con pollo*.
About my husband's hands: how they smacked

and sounded against a soft stretch of skin
the moment I began to love him.

About the censors, the just-lip
kisses, our beds: parallel plots.

About the baby – the "How?"
> (as if there wasn't the kitchen counter after
> dinner dishes, the damp bathroom floor
> before showering)

About the way my mother is always looking slightly
above my eyes when she talks to me.
Calls him Mickey. Hates the ride to see us.

About my best friend; her "no" as "yes."
About broomsticks sounding against ceilings and
grapes between your toes.

About my closet, my costume.
My pins and polish. The henna rinse. The lip stick.
And all the other ways I have chose to be
    without being.

Dream Analysis

Last night, I dreamed the man I love
ironed my heart out flat across the kitchen counter.

Wrote out his ink-dark love for me
across all four chambers, gave it back blanched

on a bed of satin –
a valentine. All schoolyard. All paste and puncture.

I grew grey at the absence. The walls lost all color.
Next, laughter: first soft from the farthest stretch of the
room then sharp –

broken plates, forks and knives hitting floor
tea kettle cackle –

I was outside of myself then.
He held me in his hand so easy,

so Morning Paper,
so Baseball.

I was my own gift, and I said "thank you" to the open
wound between my breasts.

Transcript from Session #2

My mother used to say that every man is a door,
and the work of being a woman is knowing
what sort of room you want
to end up in –

Note: all her metaphors of love involve the domestic.
Note: she never once said a thing about 'love'.

I spent a lot of time opening doors that were locked
for a reason.
I could get into any place with a spare bobby pin
and my bedroom eyes –

I thought the door I married might lead to a stage.

I thought I'd wear sunglasses all day, and ash
on a carpet someone else would clean.

I thought I would dance
or sing or act or
anything that could turn me
into a symbol of something instead
of the thing itself –

I come from a long line of women
who make men into fire escapes.

I come from a long line
of women who would not burn
in the houses of their fathers –

let me tell you about my room:

here, the dresses hang like bodies in my closet;
here, I am the one that put them there.

Here, I make a mean meatloaf every Monday;
here, ketchup is a seasoning.

Here, our beds touch twice a week;
here, I've never once talked about my father.

Here, Friday's mean canasta and spilt beer;
here, I love to lick the sticky yeast of it from his hands.

Here, in twenty-three minutes, I can make it
look like it never happened;
here, the card table folds like I do.

Rorschach

Now that —

that is definitely a pair of bongo drums,
or his own heart-sound booming against my hollow.

It's impossible to say.

Here is what I know:
whatever it is, it is firstly him.

He, the man who found the song of my name

Lucy

first low,
languid,
loose lips about to kiss before

the slice,

the syllable softened —
that snaking sound singing

through the front door
just before
things are about to get ugly,
and I'm not sure if I'll be able to get out of this alone,

Lucy –

I'm home.

Transcript from Session #3

I guess when I first heard it, it was like
that moment when all of a sudden without bleeding,
or fucking,
or giving birth
you become, unintentionally, a woman;

and you can never go back to that place you were
before it happened so you just
stand there, dumb
and brick-heavy,
waiting for whatever it was that put you here
to take you back:

my mother,
(who had never wanted to be called
anything but her own name)

looked up from the floor where she was scrubbing lye
across linoleum and motioned for me
to bring her the pail of water by my feet before she said:

"Lucille, you can't be in the show."

(Here, there is a long silence. A clearing of the throat.)

And I've always been a little bit there ever since.
Even when I'm here with you, or home
with him, I'm also there, looking at her
looking at me.

Word Association

Friend?
Ethel.

Friend. Ethel.
Ethel back door friend,

early morning curlers, coffee, kerchief friend,
Ethel bosom buddy, blonde – but still smarter than me.

Ethel Bridge games: my bridge Ethel holding me
thick armed on shoulders.

Ethel mouthful of chocolates.
Ethel mouth always full,

stretching after me, for what I've forgotten,
or lost.

Ethel lost in joke. Ethel pause for laughter.
Ethel wait to talk. Ethel "No"

Ethel "Maybe"
Ethel "Never Again"

Ethel again, and again

Ethel always here. Ethel always will be.

Always.

Transcript from Session #4

The first time I fell in love I was a brunette,
and my mother made me

take teaspoons of turpentine and lie
in the bathtub until I didn't feel it anymore.

I think I was a soft vessel then.

I think that night in the field, he only wanted to touch my hand and
I think I just wanted to belong to someone else.

(Last Wednesday, when Ricky was on top of me, he squeezed the pale bird
of my neck as he came and I thought this,
        this
                this is it –
the part of love that is swollen
and red)

Regression Therapy

3.

Soon, it will be that time of year
my grandfather was born into:
high August, sweat
in the small of the back; cherry pits
spit into wheat grass –

in a month like this, his mother's body
opened for him
pink as a promise.

The summer before he died,
he planted a grapevine
in the backyard of my childhood home.

I drank lemonade on the back porch and watched him
spread cow shit across the once-green ground;

his body is buried in a country
I may never see again.

2.

I keep coming back to the body:
How it is here, and then it is not.

On Sundays my mouth closes
around the body of Christ –
no metaphor, the priest says,
this is not a figure of speech.

Last summer I swam
in His purple blood and nearly drowned.
It stained my skin.
I fought like hell to get out.

1.

How am I supposed to tell you what it means
to eat the grapes
he planted for me? How
could you know unless you too
have loved and lost
and ate
again?

Transcript from Session #5

Someone once said that insanity was doing
the same thing over and over again
while expecting a different result.

I think this person must have been a man.
I think this person must have had a wife
who wanted too big.

I want to tell you about early morning –
when the lights aren't up yet.

When I lean my body out my bedroom window
into the thick soup
of the city, and everything is, again,
just beginning.

This is the moment right before the wish:
when he walks in about to say something that will
shatter me.

The plan before the punch line.

The air a thrown pie sails through.

The dark you sit in as the spotlight searches
for your skin

(when you are nearly nothing,
when your heart is not a poem
or a symbol or a theme song –
but an organ, that is heavy
and mostly tired.)

This is bringing teaspoon to pursed lips.

The sharp intake before the unraveling,

when I want to weep,
       but wail.

Role Play: Conversation with the Husband

Ricky: [ranting in Spanish]
Lucy: How dare you say that to me!
Ricky: What did I say?
Lucy: I don't know, but how dare you!

Last night, in the grey-dark of our room,
I heard the bongo-drum-boom of your laugh
sound from your bed when I made that joke
about your mother
tongue.

I think we fell in love in translation.
I think that first time I slept in your too-small bed
beside you, you would have rather said *te quiero*.

Who were we then?

Who were you when you cracked
your bedroom window open to let out
our heat, your beard
already growing back
from morning?

Who was I, bare-breasted,
in the blue light, wiping
my lipstick from your mouth
with the wet napkin of my skin?

How could we know what we would be
to each other now?

How could I know then that
now, when you laugh at my joke in the dark
I still see that boy, weak from loving,
falling back into bed beside me?

I'm not sure what you said,
but I know it would have wounded the girl I was then.
The girl I hold inside of me
like a lead weight.

It's all for her you know –
the girl with brown hair and bad skin,
the girl they tried to bury
beside my mother.

Afterward

"I have looked at it so long, I think it is a part of my heart"
Sylvia Plath

Ethel Mertz Reflects

I was born into a home of syrup and music.
My first words were song,
formed around the twisting veins of licorice sticks –

you see, my father sold sweets.
I can still remember the checkerboard floors
and the way he smiled at the children's faces pressed
up against the cool glass cases –

I never saw him happier
than when he washed away
their still-tapping finger prints
knowing they'd be back tomorrow,

knowing there would always be children.

My mother was taller than him,
big boned, bred on whole milk and red meats–
she taught me how to play piano in between meals.
I sat on her lap and rested my hands on hers
as they'd skid across the ivory of the keys –
my head, falling against her metronome heart.

It stopped ticking when I was twelve.

She was my father's wife.
She was born and buried in Albuquerque,
at least, that's what it says on the grey thumb
of her headstone.
It said nothing of her music.
Nothing of her early morning soprano trill,
nothing of her hands –

I began to long for something
that could no longer be found
in my mother's piano string fingers,
my father's candy heart.

I cut off all my hair and moved
to New York as soon as my father
turned plum-purple in protest.
There was always work in night clubs,
always a song that needed singing
an act that needed acting, and
I could stretch my taffy
skin and make myself be anything they wanted:

I was a dancer for sometime.

A juggler.
A magician's assistant.

A lady-clown.

I met him on a Friday night.
His body denounced him as a dancer,
but his voice –
a soft, warm tenor: peppermint sweet.
He introduced himself shyly,
wiping the sweat from his forehead,
"I'm Fred."

I knew that I would only sing again
if it was with him.

We waited too long to start a family.
My body knew better
than to try and hold the children inside of me.
The strings of my heart echoed empty
through that hollow
through that place where something
used to be.

I know it broke him.
I know he had his baseball signed
by Babe Ruth waiting on a shelf somewhere –
I know he grew bitter
only so we wouldn't grow completely apart. But,

the nursery always seemed somewhat wrong anyways.
The crib didn't fit right. The baby clothes were dated.
The children in our building grew up.
We stopped thinking about how they got there.

Then came those years,
that unassigned emptiness before there was laughter or mischief –
I put on some weight.
Dressed solely for comfort. Read a few good books.
I had friends but,
not really.

I didn't know her name for the first few days.
She lived upstairs
and whenever that man spoke it out loud
it was always slightly
slurred.
The murmur and echo

of the hallways
made everything sound underwater.

Lucy

I made her a casserole.

Lucy

We talked for hours.

Lucy

she was Technicolor
she was red
she was eyelashes
she was want
above all she was want

want of what I had had
what I had lived for years and left for no
real reason.

They never wrote in my reason.

Ricky wanted nothing
more than a good home.
He wanted what she could give him
with her Upstate comfort
her childlike virtue.
And Lucy,
well Lucy wanted what he could give her, that life
illuminated in lights
that fame –

(sometimes I wonder what made her that way she was;
what absent father, what drunken mother denied
her that love she looked for in crowds?)

They both wanted so completely
the people they could be.
They couldn't keep
their hands off each other; their lovemaking
woke Mrs. Trumble out of her sound sleeps and
so did their fights.

Neither of which you're supposed to know about,
you're not supposed to see those days that didn't end
with a simple hug or a just-lip kiss;

those nights, when they screamed at each other
a culture clash of words
sending the censors into panic
before he'd drink himself into stupor
and she'd chain smoke in the bathroom.

I only know,
because I was there.

The straight woman.
The side-kick.
The second banana.
The ass of the fat jokes.
I could play piano
       if we all felt like singing,
I could wrap chocolates
       if she asked me right.

Acknowledgements

I owe a debt of gratitude to the many people in my life who have, directly and indirectly, made this book possible:

Thank you, Paige Chaplin – my partner in poetry, my first reader. You brought me here.

Thank you, Alex Charalambides – my coach, my model for mentorship and community engagement. Your encouragement has defined my poetic voice.

Thank you, Martha Cheesman – my teacher, my coffee date therapist. You made me into the teacher who stays after school to hear new poems.

Thank you, Carrie Conlon – my mirror, my finally-found sister. I feel an inch taller every time we talk.

Thank you, Elke Nordeen – my compass, my map home. You've punctuated my existence in ways that can only be described as magic.

Thank you, Kathleen Liljegren – my grandmother, patron saint of the written word. The memory of you reading everyday at your kitchen table will stay with me forever.

Thank you, Rachael Stillman – my first friend, my Ethel. Growing up with you has been a defining joy of my life.

Thank you, Samantha St. Lawrence – my other half, my balance beam. You're the best editor I've ever had, on and off the page.

I would also like to thank Annie Pluto & Aaron Smith, my mentors – your ability to code switch between the creative and the academic inspires me endlessly.

And thank you to my parents, who gave me room to wander and wonder, and let me stay up way too late watching *I Love Lucy* reruns.

Thank you.

About the Author

Taylor Liljegren is a poet and educator from Central Massachusetts. She received her undergraduate degree in English Literature & Secondary Education from Lesley University, and is a candidate for her Masters in English Literature through the Bread Loaf School of English at Middlebury College. Her work has previously been published in *Best Indie Lit New England*, Vol. 2 (Black Key Press) as well as *Nixes Mate Review: Anthology 2016-2017*.

42° 19′ 47.9″ N   70° 56′ 43.9″ W

Nixes Mate is a navigational hazard in Boston Harbor used during the colonial period to gibbet and hang pirates and mutineers.

Nixes Mate Books features small-batch artisanal literature, created by writers who use all 26 letters of the alphabet and then some, honing their craft the time-honored way: one line at a time.

nixesmate.pub/books

www.ingramcontent.com/pod-product-compliance
Lightning Source LLC
Chambersburg PA
CBHW052106110526
44591CB00013B/2367